WHERE ARE THEY?

SEARCH FOR SANTA'S HELPERS

Fee

Fi

BY
ANTHONY TALLARICO

SMITHMARK

Copyright © 1991 Kidsbooks Inc. and Anthony Tallarico
7004 N. California Ave.
Chicago, IL 60645

This edition published in 1991 by SMITHMARK Publishers Inc.
112 Madison Avenue, New York, NY 10016

ISBN: 0-8317-7726-5

SMITHMARK books are available for bulk purchase for
sales promotion and premium use.
For details write or telephone
the Manager of Special Sales, SMITHMARK Publishers Inc.
112 Madison Avenue, New York, NY 10016   (212) 532-6600

Manufactured in the United States of America

Fo

Fun

The elves made so many gifts this year that they're running out of places in which to store them.

SEARCH FOR FEE, FI, FO, AND FUN AT THE GIFT STORAGE CENTER AND...

☒ Baseball bat
☒ Bell
☒ Book
☐ Bowling ball
☒ Candy canes (3)
☐ Clown
☒ Duck
☒ Earmuffs (2 pairs)
☒ Elves with beards (3)
☒ Empty warehouse
☒ Evergreen trees (14)
☒ Fishing pole
☒ Flower
☒ Footballs (2)
☒ Horse
☒ Igloo
☒ Jack-in-the-box
☒ Kite
☒ Lion
☒ Mouse
☒ Rabbits (2)
☒ Robot
☒ Santa Claus
☒ Scarecrow
☒ Scarves (8)
☒ Shoemaker
☒ Skier
☒ Snake
☐ Star
☒ Telescopes (2)
☐ Thermometer
☒ Toy elephants (3)
☐ Train engine
☒ Turtle
☒ Unicorn
☒ Watch

Fee	Fi
Fo	Fun

This is the place where all those fancy bows and ribbons are made.

SEARCH FOR FEE, FI, FO, AND FUN AT THE BIG BOW WORKS AND...

- ☐ Airplane
- ☐ Balloon
- ☐ Bell
- ☐ Bunny
- ☐ Cat
- ☐ Clown
- ☐ Cow
- ☐ Crayon
- ☐ Cup
- ☐ Dog
- ☐ Elephant
- ☐ Flying bat
- ☐ Garden hose
- ☐ Ghost
- ☐ Globe
- ☐ Guitar
- ☐ Hot dog
- ☐ Jack-o'-lantern
- ☐ Jack-in-the-box
- ☐ Jump rope
- ☐ Lollipops (3)
- ☐ Oil can
- ☐ Package
- ☐ Paint bucket
- ☐ Panda
- ☐ Pencil
- ☐ Piggy bank
- ☐ Robot
- ☐ Sailboat
- ☐ Snake
- ☐ Sunglasses
- ☐ Super-hero doll
- ☐ Tape measure
- ☐ Truck
- ☐ Unicorn
- ☐ Wreath
- ☐ Yellow star

Fee | Fi

Fo | Fun

"The stockings were hung by the chimney with care..."

SEARCH FOR FEE, FI, FO, AND FUN'S STOCKINGS AND...

☐ Apple
☐ Bell
☐ Birds (2)
☐ Candles (2)
☐ Candy cane
☐ Flowers (2)
☐ Football
☐ Hole in a stocking
☐ Mice (3)
☐ Santa Claus
☐ Star
☐ Suspenders
☐ Tree
☐ Turtle
☐ Wreath

If your name, or the name of anyone else you know, does not appear, write it on one of the blank stockings.

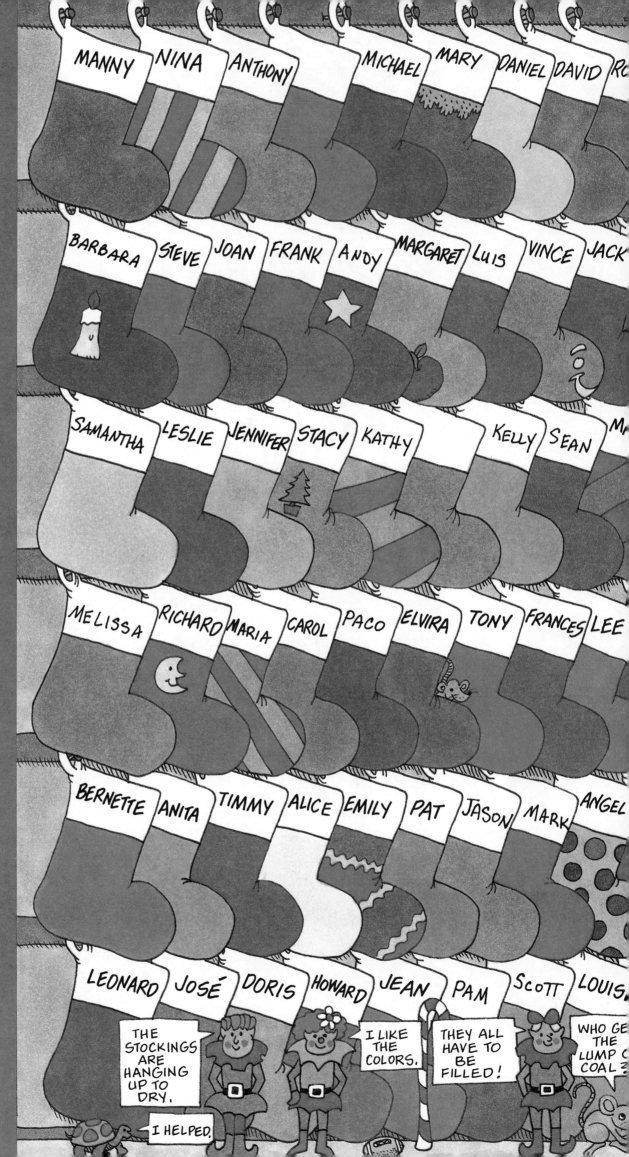

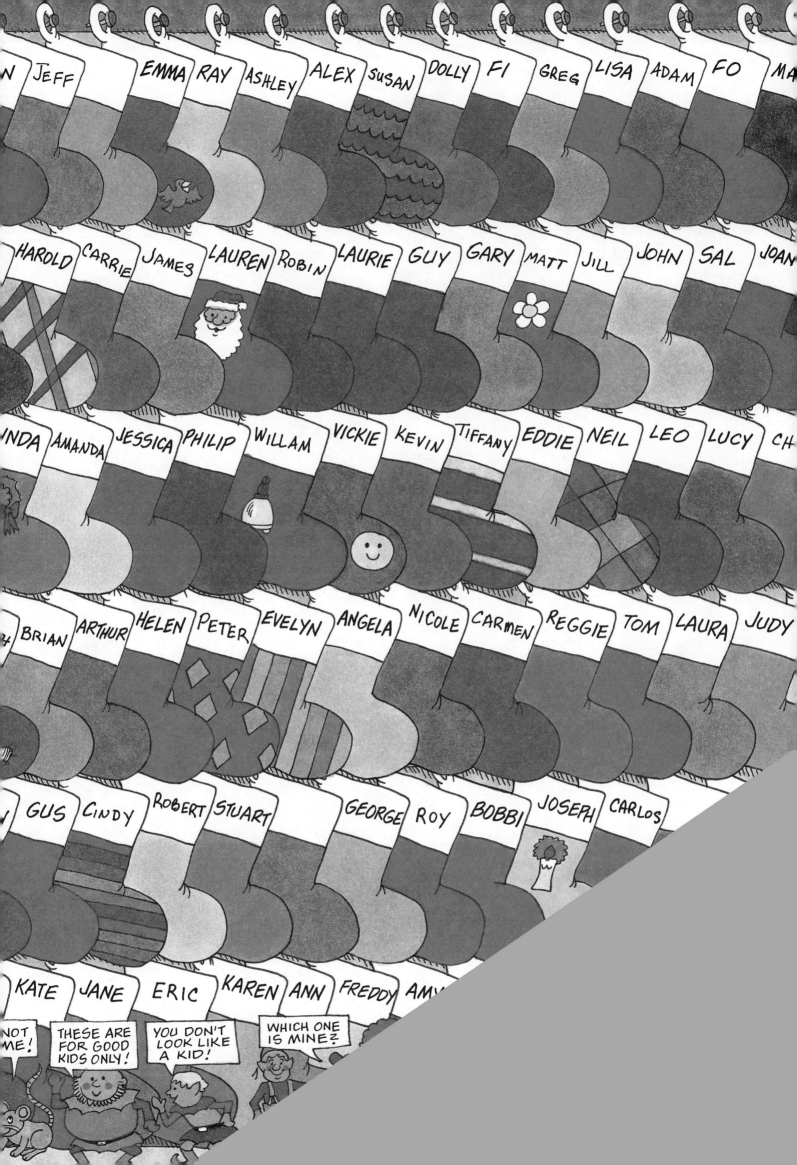

The elves are hard at work making lots of wonderful gifts for Santa to deliver on Christmas Eve.

SEARCH FOR FEE, FI, FO, AND FUN AT SANTA'S WORKSHOP AND...

- ☐ Alien spaceship
- ☐ Airplanes (2)
- ☐ Astronaut
- ☐ Banana peel
- ☐ Barbell
- ☐ Bird
- ☐ Bottle
- ☐ Bowling ball
- ☐ Broom
- ☐ Candle
- ☐ Chimneys (3)
- ☐ Clock
- ☐ Cowboy hats (7)
- ☐ Fish
- ☐ Flower
- ☐ Frog
- ☐ Green feather
- ☐ Hockey stick
- ☐ Ice skate
- ☐ Juggler
- ☐ Magnifying glass
- ☐ Mallets (2)
- ☐ Moose head
- ☐ Mouse
- ☐ Nets (3)
- ☐ Race car
- ☐ Rejected candy cane
- ☐ Rocket ship
- ☐ Rocking chair
- ☐ Saddle
- ☐ Sailor hat
- ☐ Saw
- ☐ Screw
- ☐ Skateboard
- ☐ Sock
- ☐ Surfboard
- ☐ Tent
- ☐ Toy soldier
- ☐ Tree ornaments (2)
- ☐ TV antenna

fee Fi Fo Fun

Each year the busy elves relax by running a marathon race.

SEARCH FOR FEE, FI, FO, AND FUN AT THE ANNUAL NORTH POLE RACE AND...

☐ Apple
☐ Bald elf
☐ Balloon
☐ Bed
☐ Birdhouse
☐ Boot
☐ Candle
☐ Candy canes (3)
☐ Cans (2)
☐ Cap
☐ Cherry
☐ Chimney
☐ Coffee pot
☐ Deer
☐ Duck
☐ Giraffe
☐ Igloo
☐ Jack Frost
☐ Last year's winner
☐ Number 17
☐ Painted egg
☐ Periscope
☐ Pillows (2)
☐ Rabbit
☐ Rag doll
☐ Robot
☐ Scarf
☐ Seal
☐ Shovel
☐ Skier
☐ Sled
☐ Snowman
☐ Tent
☐ Tepee
☐ Top hat
☐ Tree
☐ Umbrella
☐ Wreaths (2)
☐ Wrong-way runner

fee Fi Fo Fun

The Christmas trees are all anxious to be shipped to different places throughout the world.

SEARCH FOR FEE, FI, FO, AND FUN IN THE CHRISTMAS TREE FOREST AND...

☐ Artificial tree
☐ Ax
☐ Bandanna
☐ Baseball bat
☐ Blue spruce tree
☐ Book
☐ Boots (2 pairs)
☐ Bow tie
☐ Chef's hat
☐ Christmas stocking
☐ Cowboy hat
☐ Deer
☐ Envelope
☐ Firefighter's hat
☐ Ghost tree
☐ Hollywood tree
☐ Ice skates
☐ Kite
☐ Little Red Riding Hood
☐ Mouse
☐ Nest
☐ Package
☐ Scarecrow
☐ Scarves (3)
☐ Schoolhouse tree
☐ Sled
☐ Smallest tree
☐ Stars (2)
☐ Sunglasses
☐ Tepee
☐ Top hat
☐ Toy train
☐ Turtle
☐ Wooden shoe
☐ Walrus
☐ Wreath

Fee Fi
Fo Fun

The card makers are really busy this time of year.

SEARCH FOR FEE, FI, FO, AND FUN AT THE CHRISTMAS CARD FACTORY AND...

☐ Arrow
☐ Balloon
☐ Beachball
☐ Bird
☐ Birdhouse
☐ Bone
☐ Broom
☐ Candle
☐ Cat
☐ Chair
☐ Cloud
☐ Curtains
☐ Dog
☐ Elephant
☐ Fake snow
☐ Feather
☐ Fish
☐ Flower
☐ Hammer
☐ Heart
☐ Ice skates
☐ Igloo
☐ Kite
☐ Lights (2)
☐ Models (4)
☐ Number 26
☐ Paint bucket
☐ Paintbrush
☐ Pencil
☐ Pizza
☐ Scarf
☐ Scissors
☐ Shovels (2)
☐ Star
☐ Turtle
☐ Wagon
☐ Wreath

Everybody loves to sing Christmas songs, especially the elves.

SEARCH FOR FEE, FI, FO, AND FUN AT THE CHRISTMAS CAROL SING-ALONG AND...

- ☐ Angel
- ☐ Balloons (5)
- ☐ Baseball
- ☐ Baseball cap
- ☐ Bells (2)
- ☐ Cactus
- ☐ Candy canes (2)
- ☐ Carrot
- ☐ Christmas stockings (2)
- ☐ Clothespin
- ☐ Deer
- ☐ Dog
- ☐ Duck
- ☐ "Elfis"
- ☐ Elves wearing glasses (4)
- ☐ Elves with beards (2)
- ☐ Feather
- ☐ Flute
- ☐ Flying carpet
- ☐ Football helmet
- ☐ Horse
- ☐ Ice skates
- ☐ Jack-in-the-box
- ☐ Kettle drum
- ☐ Mouse
- ☐ Parrot
- ☐ Penguin
- ☐ Pillow
- ☐ Pizza
- ☐ Rabbits (2)
- ☐ School bag
- ☐ Singing tree
- ☐ Skier
- ☐ Stars (2)
- ☐ Torn gloves
- ☐ Tuba
- ☐ Umbrella
- ☐ Watering can
- ☐ Wreaths (3)

fee Fi Fo Fun

With a little teamwork, and a lot of elves, making wreaths is easy and fun to do.

SEARCH FOR FEE, FI, FO, AND FUN AT THE WREATH MAKERS AND...

☐ Balloon
☐ Bird
☐ Candle
☐ Candy cane
☐ Chair
☐ Christmas stockings (2)
☐ Crayon
☐ Crown
☐ Deer
☐ Doors
☐ Duck
☐ Falling star
☐ Fish
☐ Football
☐ Garden hose
☐ Ice skates
☐ Jack-in-the-box
☐ Jars of glue (3)
☐ Ladder
☐ Light bulbs (3)
☐ Mouse
☐ Oil can
☐ Paintbrush
☐ Pencils (2)
☐ Picture frame
☐ Pizza
☐ Propeller
☐ Rake
☐ Rejected wreaths
☐ Roller skates
☐ Shovel
☐ Snake
☐ Top hat
☐ Turtle
☐ TV set
☐ Umbrella
☐ Wagon
☐ Watering can

Fee | Fi | Fo | Fun

So many gifts...so little time... and they all have to be wrapped before Christmas Eve!

SEARCH FOR FEE, FI, FO, AND FUN AT THE GIFT WRAPPING DEPARTMENT AND...

Fee   Fi

Fo   Fun

'Tis the week before Christmas and, at the North Pole, not a creature is working, not even a mole. Why not? Because it's time for the elves' Christmas party!

SEARCH FOR FEE, FI, FO, AND FUN AT THE CHRISTMAS PARTY AND...

☐ Balloon
☐ Banana
☐ Bell
☐ Birds (2)
☐ Bows (4)
☐ Broom
☐ Clock
☐ Chef's hat
☐ Christmas stocking
☐ Deer
☐ Dog
☐ Dracula
☐ Eyeglasses (2 pairs)
☐ Feather
☐ Fish
☐ Flowerpot
☐ Football helmet
☐ Guitar
☐ Horn
☐ Igloo
☐ Jack-o'-lantern
☐ Loudspeaker
☐ Mama Claus
☐ Mouse
☐ Piano
☐ Pitcher
☐ Rabbit
☐ Rocking chair
☐ Roller skates (2)
☐ Scrooge
☐ Seal
☐ Snake
☐ Snowman
☐ Star
☐ Straw
☐ Top hats (2)
☐ Train engine
☐ Turtles (2)
☐ Umbrella

Fee Fi
Fo Fun

What a wonderful place to work. It looks like a delicious crop this year!

SEARCH FOR FEE, FI, FO, AND FUN AT THE CANDY CANE FARM AND...

☐ Airplane
☐ Ax
☐ Barn
☐ Barrel
☐ Baseball bat
☐ Birds (7)
☐ Broom
☐ Carrot
☐ Condo
☐ Crayon
☐ Crown
☐ Dog
☐ Elephant
☐ Evergreen tree
☐ Goat
☐ Goose
☐ Hammock
☐ Helicopter
☐ Hot dog
☐ Kangaroo
☐ Laundry
☐ Mailbox
☐ Mouse
☐ Pail
☐ Paint bucket
☐ Pencil
☐ Pig
☐ Polka-dotted cane
☐ Rabbit
☐ Reject basket
☐ Shovel
☐ Sled
☐ Snowball fight
☐ Straw hat
☐ Stripeless cane
☐ Tractor
☐ Wagon
☐ Watering can
☐ Windmill

Fee	Fi
Fo	Fun

The big night—
Christmas Eve—is
finally here!
Everyone is helping
to pack the sleigh,
and Santa is ready
to go!

SEARCH FOR FEE,
FI, FO, AND FUN
ON CHRISTMAS
EVE AND...

☐ Apple
☐ Arrow
☐ Baseball
☐ Basket
☐ Bell
☐ Boots (2 pairs)
☐ Bunny
☐ Camera
☐ Candelabra
☐ Crayons (3)
☐ Drum
☐ Earmuffs
☐ Envelope
☐ Hockey stick
☐ Hoe
☐ Horn
☐ Igloo
☐ Iron
☐ Knitting needles
☐ Lollipop
☐ Old-fashioned
   radio
☐ Picture frame
☐ Polka-dotted bow
☐ Propellers (2)
☐ Robot
☐ Sailboat
☐ Shovel
☐ Slide
☐ Stars (3)
☐ Stowaway
☐ Sunglasses
   (2 pairs)
☐ Toaster
☐ Top hat
☐ Train engines (2)
☐ Umbrella
☐ Wagon
☐ Weather vane
☐ Wheelbarrow
☐ Wreath

LOTS OF GREETINGS- LAURA

I DETECT- CHRISTMAS! DONALD

from- FEE

SEASON'S BEST! SUSIE

MERRY CHRISTMAS- FRANKIE

from- FI

LOTS OF CHEER LISA

HAVE A HOPPY TIME! BUNNY HONEY

HO-HO-HO-HO-HO

from- FO

SEASON'S GREETINGS SAM

GREETINGS- FREDDIE

HAVE A HAPPY HECTOR

HAVE FUN- FUN

Christmas greetings to you from Fee, Fi, Fo, Fun, and their friends:

Freddie   Hector
Lisa   Laura
Susie   Santa
Frankie   Donald
Bunny Honey   Sam

SEARCH FOR SANTA'S HELPERS